Happy Halloween!

Sticker Doodle Boo!

HOW DO YOU DOODLE DO?

Doodling is very easy AND fun! Just pick up your pen, and DRAW, squiggle, zigzag or scribble!

Do whatever you want to!

I'm Doodle Monster. Look out for me, inside!

priddy books

big ideas for little people

Give this pumpkin a really scary face!

Spooky!

Pumpkin head

Doodle a face, arms, and big jaws!

Is this
the scariest
monster ever?

Scary monster

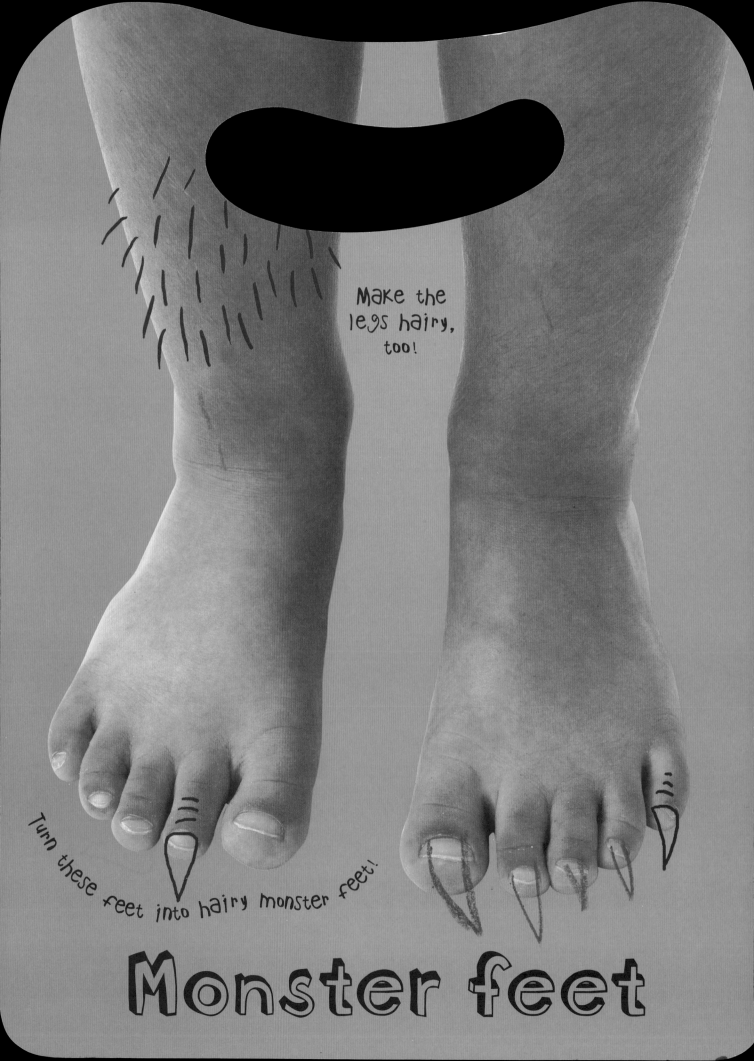

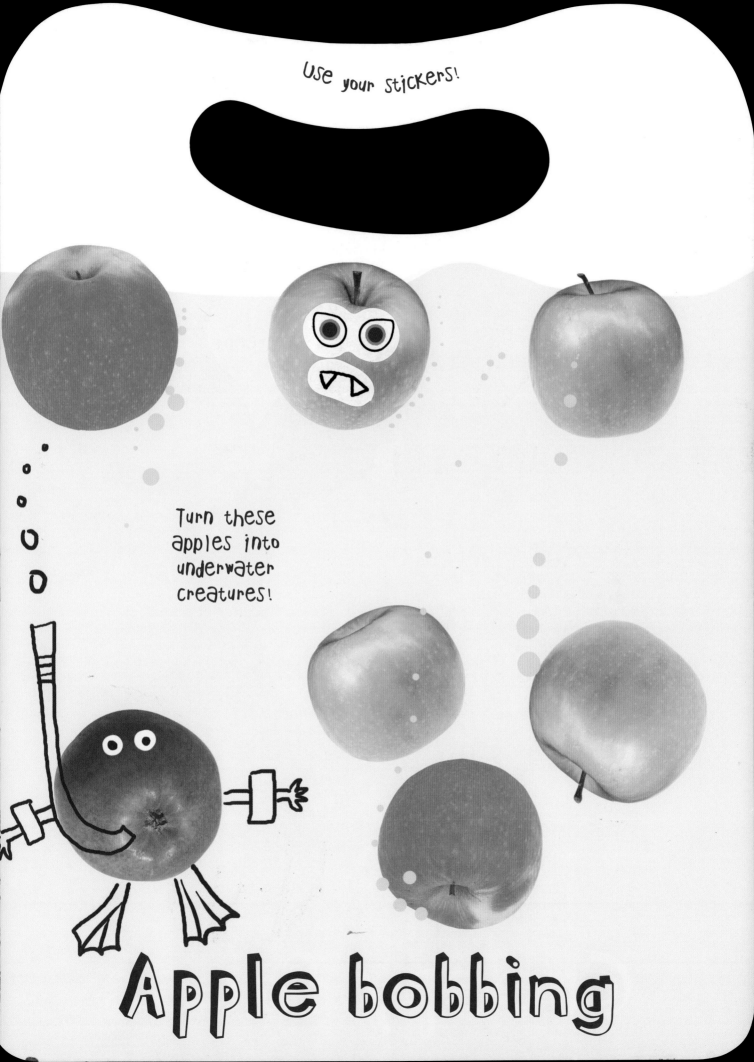

Use your stickers!

Turn these
apples into
underwater
creatures!

Apple bobbing

Sweet spiders

Give these skeletons some boney bodies.

Boney buddies

This sinister skeleton needs some skeletal features!

Hi, I'm Suzy Skeleton. I like to scream loudly!

Suzy Skeleton

Decorate this house and make it ready for Halloween night!

Happy Halloween

Halloween house

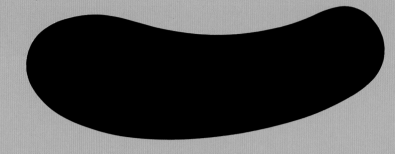

Fill the jars with mischievous Halloween candies.

Halloween candies

Draw the scariest thing you can think of.

Don't draw me!

Scariest doodle

Doodle some sp👀ky friends in the eerie forest.

Eerie forest

Turn these everyday things into evil masterminds.

Snap!

Snap!
Snap!

Evil objects

Spooky patterns

Turn the frosting on the cupcakes into scary little ghouls.

Cupcake ghosts

Draw spooky shadows in the windows of the Haunted House!

Use your stickers!

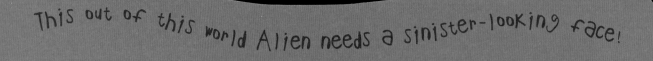

This out of this world Alien needs a sinister-looking face!

Hi, I'm Annie Alien. I like to zap things!

Annie Alien

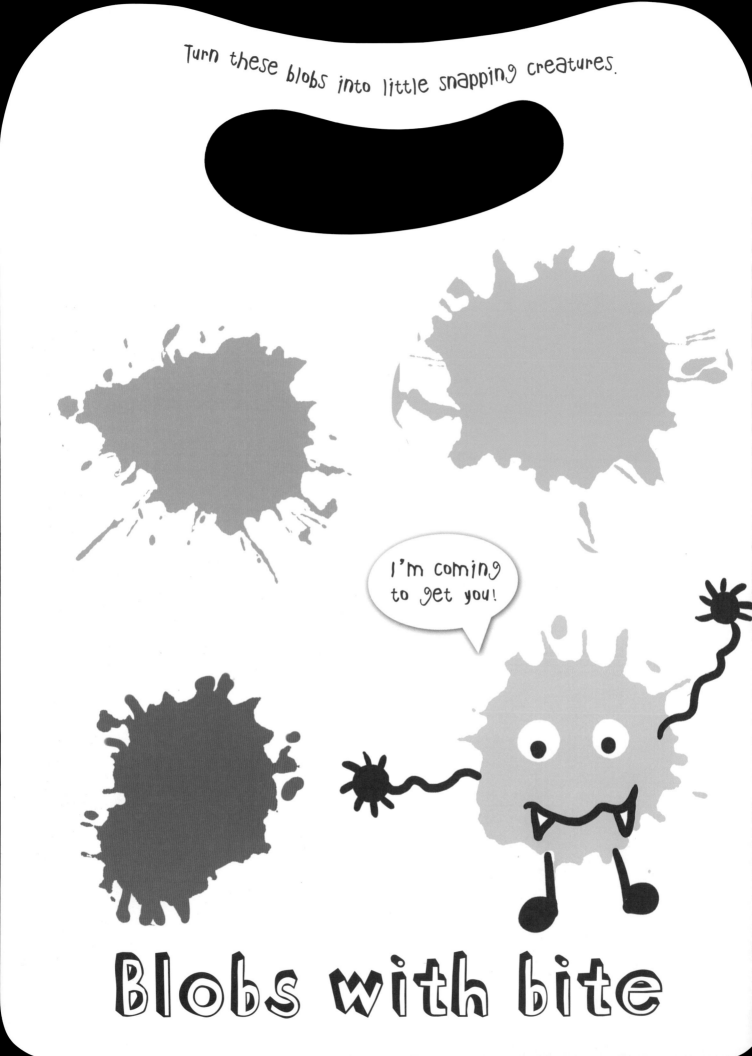

Doodle more witches and cats flying through the night sky.

Add more stars!

Witches and cats

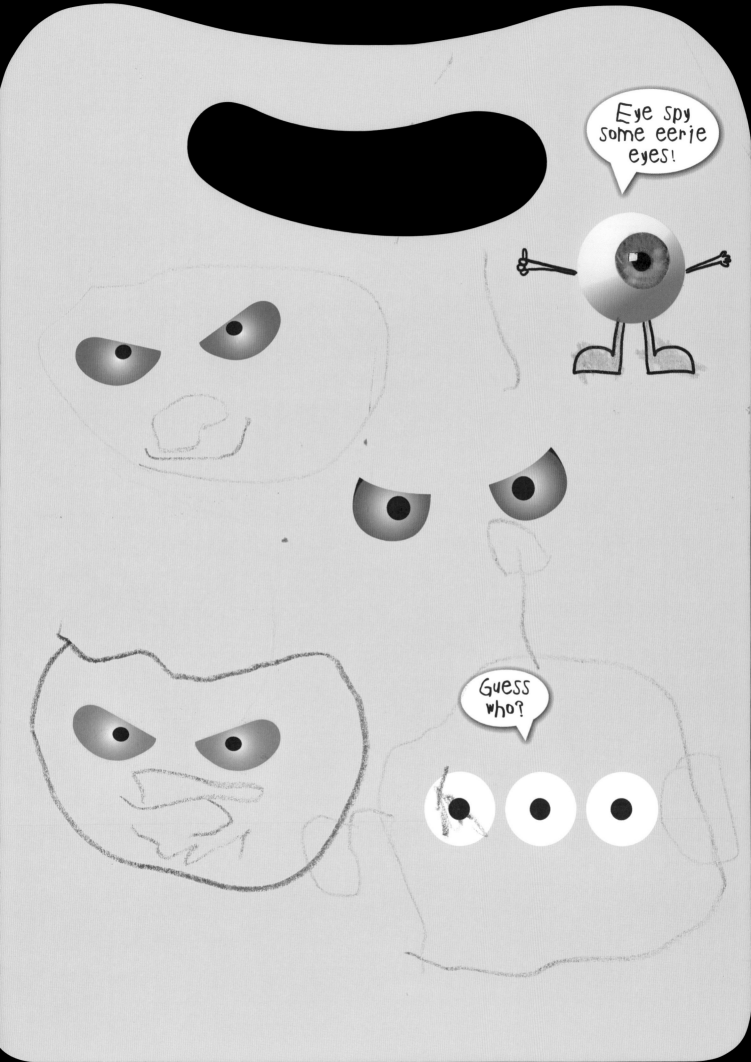

Scary patterns

Turn these buttons into shrieking creatures.

Boo to you, too!

Boo!

Boo!

Boo!

Boo buttons

Turn these knotted handkerchiefs into bats.

They're knot bats

Doodle the items from the spell menu dropping into the cauldron!

Spell Menu

Werewolf's hair
Witch's toe
Zombie's snot
Monster's puke
Vampire's fang
Frog's breath

Spell cauldron

Doodle a face, arms, and more hair!

Give this monster a name!

Hairy monster

Keep drawing round and round this skull!

Skull face

Add some disgusting toppings to this pizza!

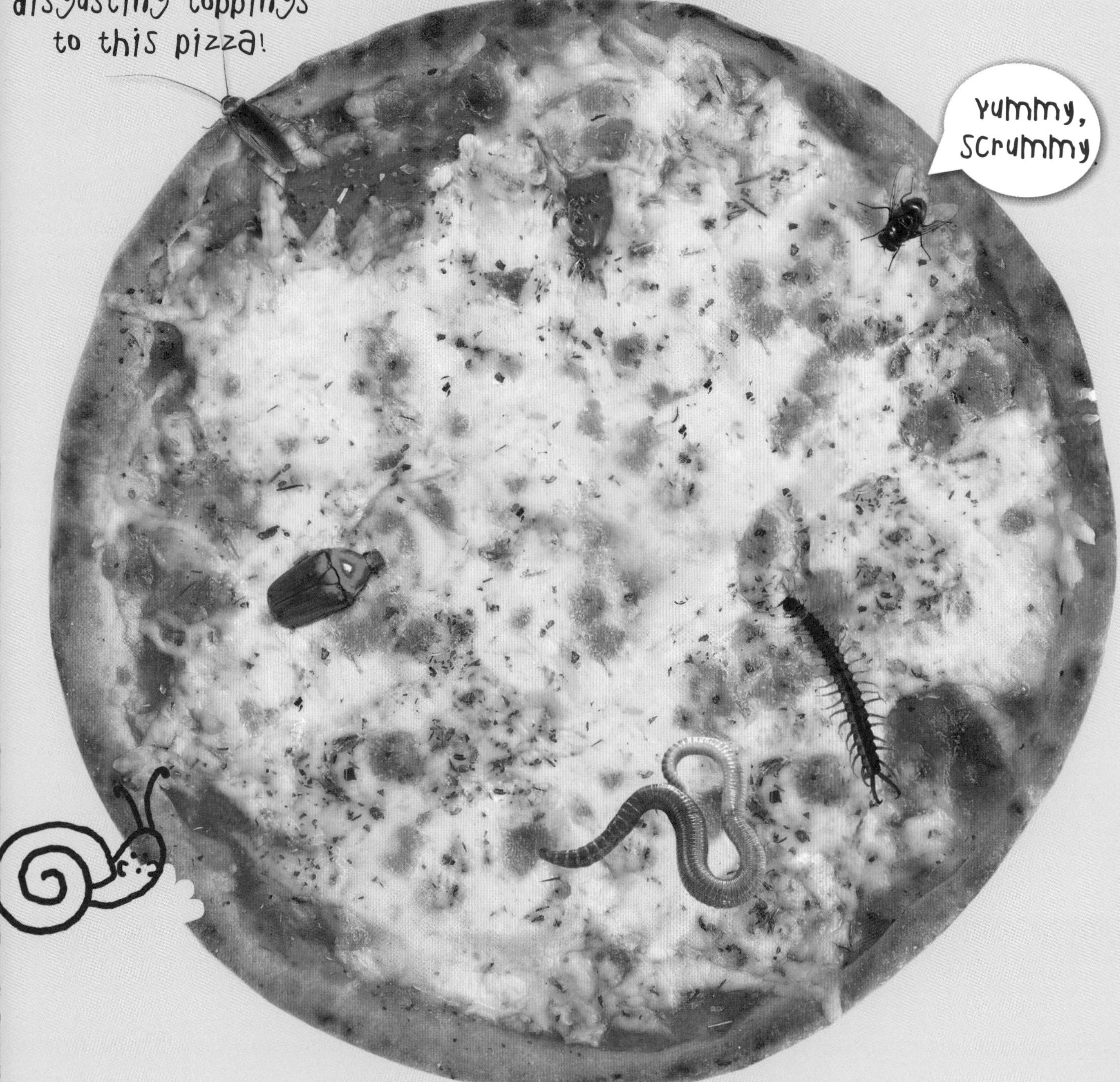

Pukey pizza

Keep drawing around this pumpkin!

I'm a cool purple ghoul!

Pumpkin pattern

Burp!

Fill this school bus with ghouls and goblin creatures of the night.

Spooky bus

Turn these fruits into freaky creatures!

Freaky fruit

What creatures can you doodle crawling in the witch's hair?

Hair scare

What can you doodle inside the creepy cupboard?

Creepy cupboard

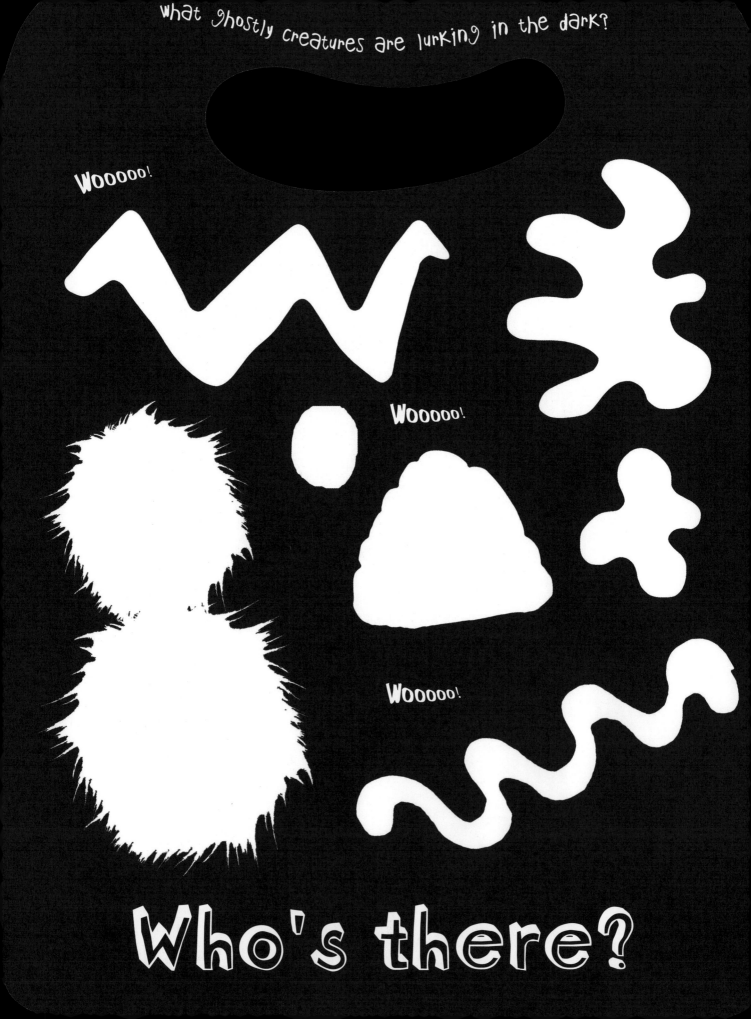

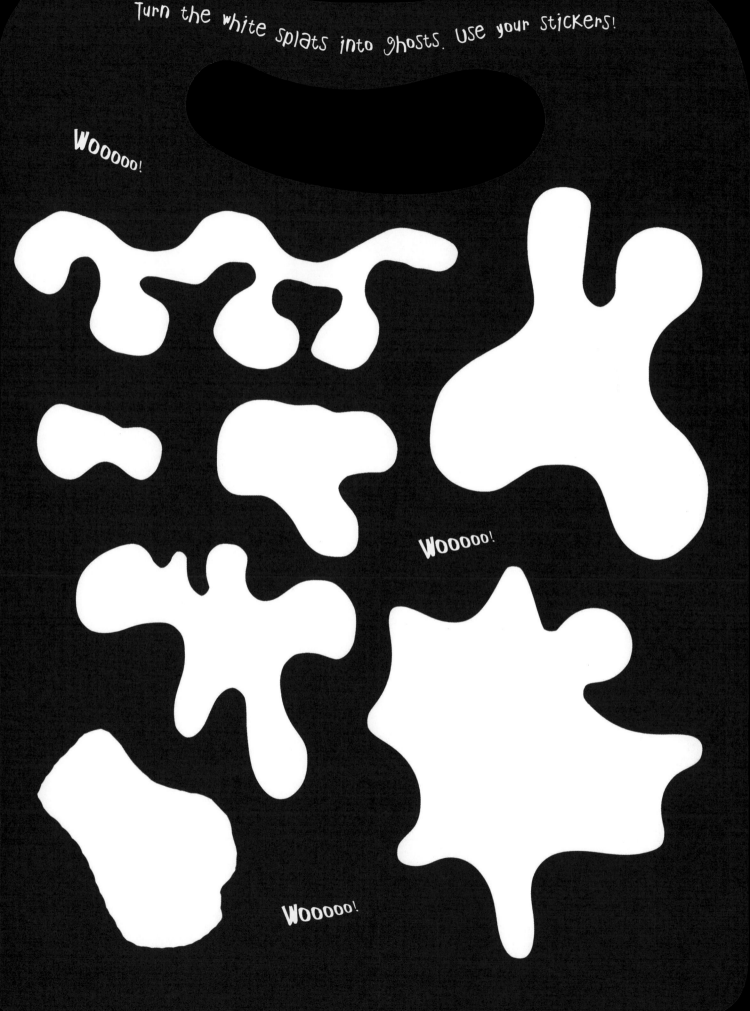

Complete these doodle patterns if you dare!

Spooky patterns

Doodle the spell
that this witch
is casting!

Which witch spell?

Doodle a spooky spectre on this broomstick.

Night flight

Doodle more spikes on this seriously spiked monster.

Give this
monster a name!

Spiked monster

Yucky milkshake

Doodle things into the glass to make this milkshake yucky!

what creatures are
flying around the
moon tonight?

use your stickers!

Dark night

Check these out!

Give these hands monster claws.

Sharp claws

Fill this page with gruesome eyeballs!

Eye eye!

Eyes everywhere.

Turn these boxes into Frankenstein heads!

Franken-boxes

Make these candies sssseriously sssnake-like!

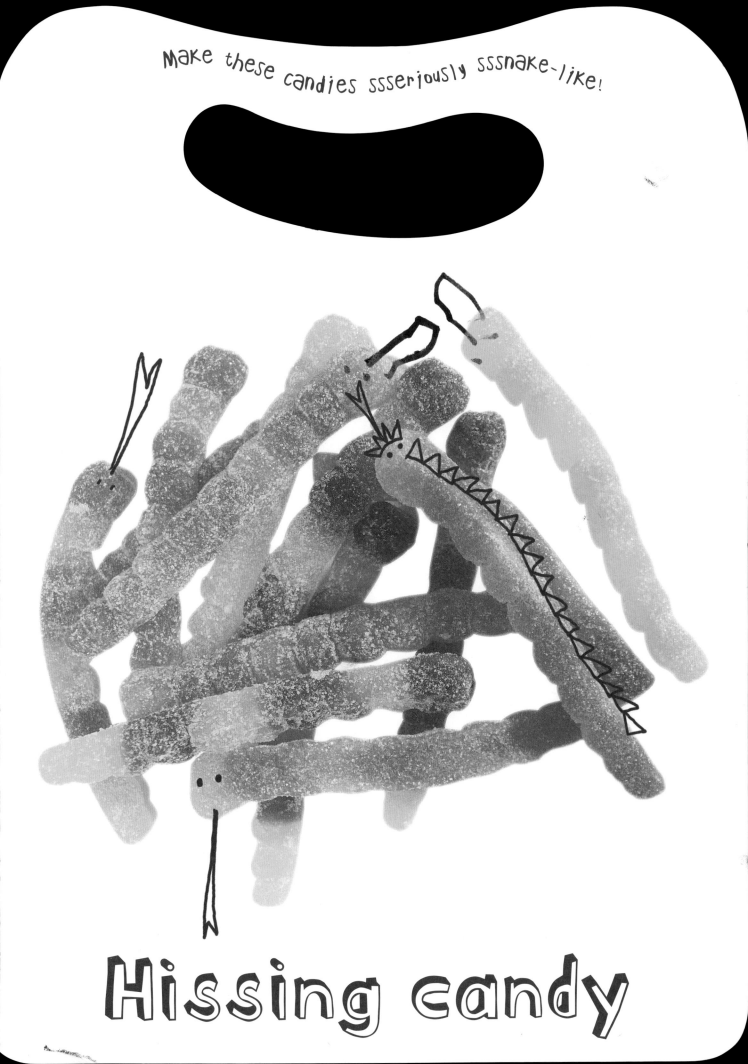

Hissing candy